How to Make Your Own Vi

M. Usman

Entrepreneur Series

Mendon Cottage Books

JD-Biz Publishing

Entrepreneur Book Series

Our books are available at

1. Amazon.com
2. Barnes and Noble
3. Itunes
4. Kobo
5. Smashwords
6. Google Play Books

Table of Contents

Preface

If you are an avid gamer, you probably have had the will to create your own game. Unfortunately, you had no idea where to start from. In this book, you will discover how you can make a game. Your ideas should not be buried in your head; you just don't know if they could make the next "Grand Theft Auto."

In order to make a simple game, you mainly need a computer and game-making software. Since you play games all the time, then you already have a computer. If not, you can build one easily. As for the softwares, you can download them online. Some are free while some come at a cost.

Making your first game will not be an easy task as there are a couple of things you need to learn first. So you should not have high hopes for your first game. But with time and practice, you will definitely get better.

In this book, I will show you the best softwares you can use to make your own games. I will also give you things you must think about before you start developing your game. In addition to that, you will also find guidance on testing your game, tips for becoming a great game developer, advice on creating game ideas, and more.

If you thought that making games was something only for big companies, this book will show you that you too can do it.

I hope you will find this book helpful.

Chapter # 1: Important Tips to Think About Before Making Your Game

You have been dreaming about your game every night. You are convinced that once it's out, it will be a hit. You see yourself making a lot of money once you release it.

However, before you go on with your aspirations, there are some important things you must take care of before you start making the game. Ignoring these may prove costly later on.

So without wasting any time, here is what you should know:

Have a Concrete Idea – It's amazing to see how many people go head-first and start developing a game without knowing what they want to achieve in the end.

Having an idea in your mind is not enough, you need to put it on paper. And when you do, take some time to look at it.

What does it make you think? Do you believe you can make good game out of this? Is it something that has already been done? Is there anything else you might add to this idea that will improve it?

A well thought-out idea acts like a lighthouse to guide you in the troubled waters. It is your railroad to keep you on track until you reach your destination.

When you have clearly defined your game idea, the steps that follow become easy.

Determine Your Audience – If only it was easy, then I would advise you to make a game for everyone. Unfortunately, that is not possible. There is no one on earth who can please everyone. With that in mind, clearly identify who will be playing your game.

Once you do, you will be in a better position to understand what makes a great game in the eyes of your audience. So you will be able to add what you know they will want to see in the game.

At the same time, you will know which platform they use mostly to play their games. For example, you may discover that your audience likes to play on mobile phones. So you will not waste your time making the game playable on an Xbox.

When your game is focused on just a single audience, chances of success are high.

Consider Your Platform – As you saw in the previous point, determining your audience makes it easy to choose a platform. Developing a game that will work on PCs, mobile phones, consoles, and other devices is not easy. It takes a lot of time, and most importantly, a lot of money. And if you are an indie developer, this is definitely a road you do not want to go.

So focus on making a game for a single platform. When doing this, keep your goal in mind. At the same time, go for a platform that your intended audience uses. Lastly, make sure you have the resources to make a successful game on this platform.

With the rise of mobile phones and an improvement in their capabilities, most games these days are being made for mobile phones. But that does not mean that PCs and consoles are dead.

Pick a Genre – No matter how creative your game is, it will still belong to some genre. You might think this is not important, but you will realize that it is when it's time to pick the right category for your game. And this is important if you are going to put it in stores for sale.

Additionally, your game has a better chance of being found by people who love to play games in the category you have chosen.

So think if yours is about racing, shooting, arcade, strategy, puzzle, etc.

Have a Great Title – People will decide to buy or download your game after reading its title. So if it does not sound promising, they will not find the motivation to read the description. And you can bet they will not even bother to click the download button.

You must remember that there are a lot of games on the market. You shouldn't cross your fingers and hope that someone will pick your game; miracles don't happen all the time. So try to give it the best title you can come up with.

Firstly, write your goal on a piece of paper. Then think of your audience and what makes a great game title to them.

Come up with a few titles and make sure that you write all of them down.

Go through a couple of them and see which ones you think will do justice to your game. If you find this process difficult, leave the titles and come back to them later. You have no need to rush.

You can also work with a couple of friends at this stage. Brainstorm title ideas and select the ones you think are great.

Additionally, you can see some game titles that are doing well and find what is common about them.

Work on Gameplay – Every game needs to progress from the time the player starts playing it. So think of what it is that the player must accomplish at each stage.

At the same time, add incentives to keep your player happy that he is conquering the challenges you set for him. To get more on this, look at other games and critically think about what it is you love about them.

You are not supposed to have everything pixel perfect at this stage. You just need to have a complete skeleton to make it easy to fill in the fresh when you start developing the game.

Be Realistic – Lastly, you must keep your dreams in touch with reality. I understand you believe that your idea is great. But the truth is that success in the game industry does not come easy. There is a lot of competition and it takes time for a beginner to make a polished game.

But this is not meant to discourage you. With hard work and a lot of practice, you can become very successful. Just don't stop at one game. Keep making more after your first one.

Chapter # 2: Coming up with Game Ideas

Generating a great game idea is not easy. Sitting in your room waiting for it to fall from the ceiling will not get you anywhere. You have to actively seek it. This means that every day, you must dedicate time just to come up with game ideas.

If you want to make a hit, you must create game ideas all the time. If you do this, you will land on one that will transform your life.

Here are some tips you can use to make game ideas:

Read Books – As a game developer, do not limit yourself to games as your only source of inspiration. Fiction books, as well non-fiction ones, are full of great stories that can be turned into great games. So read a lot and always be on the lookout for an idea. It's even better if you read books in every genre that you can find.

Get Ideas From Movies – There are a lot of games that have been inspired by movies. But that does not mean you must copy the movie or you will only buy yourself trouble. Instead, think of how you can present the story in the movie from a new angle. For example, think of how it would be like if the characters in the movie had certain characteristics. Whatever comes to mind, write it down – this is not the time to be making judgments.

Use Other Games – Have you ever played a game and thought of how great it would be if something happened differently? If yes, then you already have a game idea. This does not mean you will end up with something that is so much like the inspiring-game.

Mix Different Ideas – In case you have several ideas that do not seem to make good games on their own, then try combining them. However, this is easier said than done. But if you can do it, you can end up with something great.

Day Dream – Close your eyes and let your mind go. Let it travel to a world you have never been to. Let it do whatever it wants to do. Let it create obstacles for itself. You should try to not control yourself as you do this. If you are finding the experience enjoyable, see if you can make a game out of it.

Brainstorm with Your Friends – If you have friends who like playing games, there is a good chance that they have game ideas you can use. So sit with them and start brainstorming.

Pay Attention to Your Life – By watching how you or other people live, you can come up with ideas you can use to make a game. It could be that your uncle is a truck driver. Why can't you make a game about that? Show people the challenges he meets as a truck driver. Think outside the box to make it fun.

Making a game that turns out to be a hit takes time. If you stop at one, you won't have much of a chance of ever having a great game. This is why you must have lots of games ideas so that you create new games all the time.

Chapter # 3: Choosing an Engine

No matter what kind of a game you are trying to make, you will need to have an engine. This is simply a software that enables you create everything you need about the game from scratch, to the point it is fully finished. An engine is what you use to build a world, characters, sounds, and more.

If you have the tools, you can create your own engine. In fact, it is what most big game developers do. Unfortunately, you probably do not have the luxury of a dozen developers working for you or a gargantuan budget to support such a project.

So that leaves you with one option – use engines that are already available. Some of these are paid while others are free.

Since there are a lot of them, you will need to choose one that you know will be suitable for you and your situation. Mostly, the type of game you are trying to develop and your level of expertise will determine your choice. Additionally, money may also be a deciding factor.

Each of the engines below have strengths and weakness. So you may have to do a bit of research before making your selection.

Stencyl

If you have never developed a game before, Stencyl is a good engine you can use to hone your skills. It is so easy to learn and there are a lot of tutorials to help you get started with it. Making it even better, it does not require much code. Mostly, it's drag and drop.

With some effort, you can make good games in Stencyl that can be played on Windows, Mac, Linux Android, and iOS. But if you want you games on consoles, I am afraid this is not the engine that will make that happen.

The biggest drawback with this engine is that you cannot make anything advanced. But considering that it is meant for beginners, it is not a surprise at all. If you are looking forward to make your first game, you will find Stencyl adequate.

GameMaker

If you want something that is more advanced than Stencyl, then you can go for GameMaker. Making it a good choice is that you get it for free. Just like with Stencyl, GameMaker is also suitable for beginners. It is easy to learn and there are a lot of tutorials for it on the internet.

Games in this engine are also mostly made by dragging and dropping. However, you may need to know a bit about coding to get started. You can play the games on Windows, Mac, iOS, and Android.

GameMaker is used by a lot of people and it is very popular when it comes to making 2D games.

Unity

This is a more advanced engine than the two we just looked at. It makes both 3D and 2D games, and for every platform. Once you have learned its ins and outs, you can make breath-taking games in Unity.

As with the previous two engines, there are also tutorials for this engine. If you have never made a game before, I recommend that you take some time studying these.

Unity is probably the most popular engine that there is. And that's because it works.

Unreal Engine

If you never thought that you could make stunning games with your average tools, then Unreal Engine is here to show you that you can. As long as you have a good idea and have figured out everything else to make the game great, this engine can bring your imagination to life.

Unreal Engine has a lot of features. Almost everything you can ask for is present in this engine. However, that also means that you will need to spend a lot of time learning the features.

The games you can make can be played on Windows, Linux, Mac, iOS, Android, Xbox One, and Play Station 4.

A lot of good games have been made with this engine and you too can take advantage of its power.

RPG Maker VX

If you are into RPG, then this is an engine that will get your interest. Although it does not make cool games like Unity or Unreal Engine, you can still make good games with it if you let your mind think freely.

You will find that the engine is so easy to learn that even kids can use it to make their own game. At the same time, if you are a pro, you will also find that this engine has good tools you may need.

Making it better is that it's also mostly drag and drop. There is a free version you can use if you do not have a lot of money. But at the same time, there is also a paying version that gives you more features.

Once you have chosen your engine, take time to learn everything about it. You do not want to be stuck mid-way not knowing how to proceed. Since I am assuming that you have no experience in making games, the amount time you will need to spend learning will probably be a lot.

If you have a friend who knows how to use any of these engines, approach him/her and ask him/her to help you master the skills of making a game. Learning something is not always fun, especially if you have a great game idea waiting in your head. But understand that this is something you must do for a successful outcome.

Chapter # 4: Secrets on How to Make a Game Great

If truth be told, it's not every game released that is great. For the majority of game developers, creating a lovely game is a hit-or-miss affair.

Developing a good game requires that you give it your all. You must work hard at it. However, that doesn't still guarantee that you will have a good game.

Through observation, I noticed that there are some aspects common in most successful games. If you can use these when developing your own, you can be sure that you will have something good.

Small Learning Curve
No matter what kind of a game you have, you will need to teach your players how to play it. You can use whatever method you see fit to achieve

this. But what you must know is that the player should clearly understand the instructions from the get-go.

Most game developers make first levels easy to finish. This is important as it gives the player time to get acquainted with the game.

If the player has to feel like he is climbing a hill in the first levels, you will lose him.

Continuous Challenges

What would you feel like to play a game where all the levels are similar? My guess is that you wouldn't be eager to see what the last level looks like. In light of this, you must ensure that your game is filled with new challenges all the way. You do not want to bore the player by making him know what he will encounter in the next stage.

But at the same time, the challenges must not be so difficult to achieve. His eyes must not bleed just for trying to get to the end.

Set Appropriate Rewards

For each challenge you set for your player, you must have an appropriate reward for it. Otherwise, he will not find any motivation to fulfill the challenges. Rewards can come in form of bonuses, new tools he can use to excel in the game, and more.

Rewards show acknowledgment that the player did something great and he deserves to be paid for it. So when he gets to the next challenge, he is determined to succeed just to see how much you will repay his effort.

Freedom to Make Decisions

If your game feels like a one-way street, your player will surely get bored faster than you can imagine. A player must be given a chance to make decisions that affect him, otherwise, he will find the game boring. So as a developer, make sure that you give him options from time to time. Should he either take the bus or the train?

These kinds of options make the player feel like he is in control. They make him explore the world in the game.

Don't Just Focus on the Story, But Gameplay as Well

Seasoned game developers will tell you that you must focus on making great stories. And this is true. However, if you would look closely, some successful games do not have great story lines. Nevertheless, they are successful games. Angry Birds is an example of such a game. If you look at it closely, you will see that it is its gameplay that does the magic.

So make sure that you focus on both the story, as well as its gameplay.

Chapter # 5: Testing Your Game

Since this is probably your first game, you cannot rule out the possibility of imperfections. It may be that players find it difficult to understand what to do when playing. Or it may happen that it does not work flawlessly on some platforms. So it is important that before you get it to the public, you test it.

Considering that you may not have a lot of resources, you need to be strategic with how you approach this process. But that does not mean your testing should be flawed.

Many more games are being developed now than ever before. For you, this is bad news. Your players have a lot of options at their fingertips. If your game does not make the right impression from the start, know that you have lost them.

But if you take time to test it, you can improve your chances. Here is how you must do it:

Think of What You Want to Know After Testing – Before you start the testing process, clearly define what flaws you want to know about the game. Do you want to find out if the game is understandable? Or do you want to know what aspects of the game players hate? Do you want to discover what level do players stop playing?

Having this clearly defined in this phase will make everything else that follows easy.

Test on Every Platform – You must ensure that you test the game on every platform that it will be available on. Will it only be available on iOS and Android? Or do you only want it on windows and Linux? If so, you must make sure that you test it on all platforms it will be on.

Many new game developers think that if a game is working well on one platform, then it will run perfectly on all other platforms. But this is not always the case.

Use Your Friends – You should get as many people as you can to test your game. Unfortunately, to avoid disappointing you, some will tell you that the game is great when they know that it can be improved. So involve only friends you know will tell you the truth and not just what you want to hear.

Ask people Online – There are a lot of websites where you can ask people to test your game. Be sure to tell them that this is a beta. You will be surprised with how constructive some of the criticisms can be.

Your Presence During Testing

There is much debate on this topic. Some say you must be present when people are testing your game while others say you shouldn't.

Those who say you should believe that your presence influences the player's ability which may lead to an outcome you do not want. But at the same time, they say it is helpful in that you can make observations that the player will forget to tell you when he finishes playing.

Whether you watch your players test your game or not is a matter of preference. Both approaches have strengths and weaknesses.

However, if you are present during testing, make sure that you do not assist the players. Game instructions are supposed to do that. At the same time, when they are telling you how they saw the game, never interrupt them. And do not show emotion on your face; It may influence what they say which is what you are trying to avoid.

Chapter # 6: How to Promote a Game

There was a time when the word "Marketing" did not exist in a game developer's dictionary. But with time, things changed. Everybody started making games and before we knew it, the market was having game releases almost every day. This led to stiff competition.

All that brings us to one thing - if you want to make it in this industry, you must be good at marketing. Although most game developers do not love this, it is still something you must do if you want to be successful. Making it even worse is that marketing has never been easy.

So how do you go about it?

Here is how:

Begin Marketing Before the Release Date – Most games sell mainly in the first week of their release. So if you wait till the game is finished to start marketing it, you will have an extremely hard time. You will not manage to reach many people in time. And even if you could, it is a big expense all at once.

So start marketing before the release date. Your fans will be salivating at the mention of your game. Just try to create enough hype.

Have a Website – The best way to notify people about your upcoming game is by having a website. This is like having your own stand at a trade show where you have the opportunity to showcase your work. You can post updates you have made to the game, new features you believe people will enjoy, screenshots, and more.

Don't Forget Social Media – Another thing that must be included in your promotional campaign is social media. Although there are a lot of these websites, I wouldn't recommend joining all of them. Otherwise, you will go from being a game developer to a social media marketer. I would only advise that you have an account on Facebook, Twitter, and Youtube. If you believe these will not do it, then you are free to join other social networks. Just do get too much on your plate that you start spending all your time on social media sites.

Join Forums – Find one with people who love playing games and create some hype there. If you do it right, you can also get lots of visitors to your website this way. Just be careful not to overdo it to avoid being labeled as a spammer.

Tell Your Friends – You probably have some friends who love playing games. Use them to spread the word to others that your game is worth playing.

Connect with other Developers – Connecting with other like-minded people will help you get discovered and take your game development skills to new heights. You can meet these people through blogs that focus on games or any other place. And do not limit yourself to the internet; there are some good developers near where you live.

Chapter # 7: How To Become a Great Game Developer

The path to success in the gaming industry is not easy. You must overcome a lot of challenges to find your way to the top. If you work hard and rise every time you fall, your dream of becoming successful can be realized.

Below are some of the steps that will help you become a great game developer:

Play many video games – If you want to be among the best in the gaming industry, you must play a lot of games. As you do this, study what each game has that makes you fall in love with it or hate it; think of what you can do to make each game you play better.

Unfortunately, analyzing a game while playing it takes the fun out it. But it's something you need to do, nonetheless.

Understanding how other game developers make their games will equip you with a lot of knowledge. You will learn things that make games great and you will also know mistakes you must avoid.

Don't Wait for Motivation – If you wait for motivation to start making games, your chances of becoming a great game developer will be slim. Motivation does not come daily, and sometimes, you may even go for weeks without feeling it.

With this in mind, you must force yourself to develop games even when you are not feeling motivated. Sometimes, motivation comes when you just start doing something.

Learn Programming – With today's technology, you can have an acceptable game without much knowledge about coding. If you want to be the best, however, you cannot rely on basic programming knowledge - you need to be good at it.

So start learning to program right now. It's boring and intimidating at first, but once you start getting the hang of it, you will see that it is not so difficult.

Take Criticism – An extra set of eyes reviewing your work is worth its weight in gold. It will see your game from another perspective and point out flaws you may have ignored. But it is your ability to take criticism that will determine the success of this process. Whether the criticism is constructive or destructive, you must take it with a smile on your face.

You must not let yourself go blind and ignore what others are saying.

Work with Other People – The best way to hone your skills is by working with people who are good at that thing. So find programmers who are good at making games and work with them. If you can't, even a beginner will be helpful. By working in a team, you will learn things that you have yet to master. Additionally, if you go weak, your team will help you get back up.

Work on Deadlines – By setting deadlines to finish making your game, you will be forced to work at it until you finish it. But as you will be doing this, you will increase your knowledge on making games.

Conclusion

I hope the book helped you learn how you can make your own game. Having reached this far, I am sure you are now ready to put your idea into reality.

Remember to choose an engine that you know will be suitable for you. And when you do, learn all you can about it. If you know someone who is experienced in using that engine, working with him/her can be helpful to you.

The most important thing, however, is to keep working hard. You must continue to make games and not just stop at one. Perfecting your skills will take a time and lots of practice. So keep at it and you will succeed. You must strive to make every new game better than your last one.

Another important tip to keep in your mind is that you must keep studying games from other developers because we all learn from others. At the same time, be willing to take criticism from people, it's an opportunity for you to grow. If you can find other people who would like to work with you, agree. You will learn new skills.

About the Author

Dr. Usman is an MD, now pursuing his post-graduation degree. As a medical doctor, he has deep insight in all aspects of health, fitness and nutrition.

He is a certified nutritionist and a personal trainer. With these qualifications, he has helped countless people reach their health, fitness and weight loss goals.

Dr. Usman is an avid researcher with 20+ publications in internationally accepted peer reviewed journals.

He is an accomplished writer with more than 5 years of writing experience. In this time, he has produced countless blogs, articles and research work on topics related to health, fitness and nutrition.

He is a published author with more than 100+ books published and several more in the pipe line.

Finally, he runs his own blog and posts health, fitness and nutrition related articles there regularly. You can visit his blog at http://hcures.com/

Check out some of the other JD-Biz Publishing books
Gardening Series on Amazon

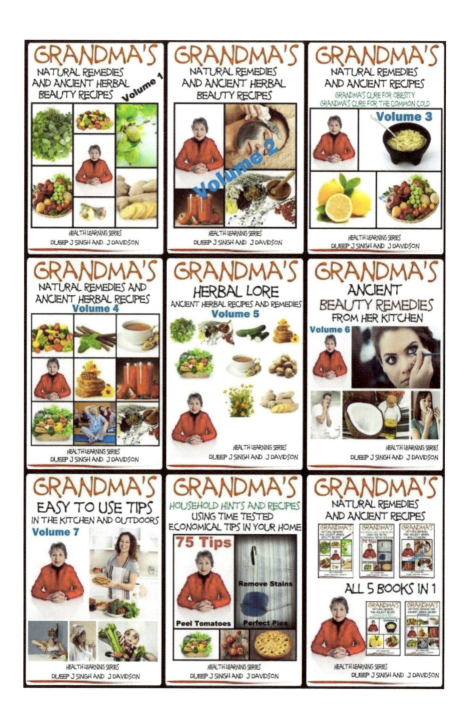

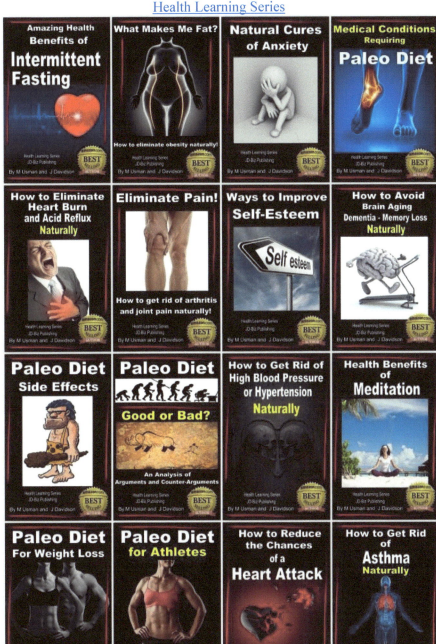

Learn To Draw Series

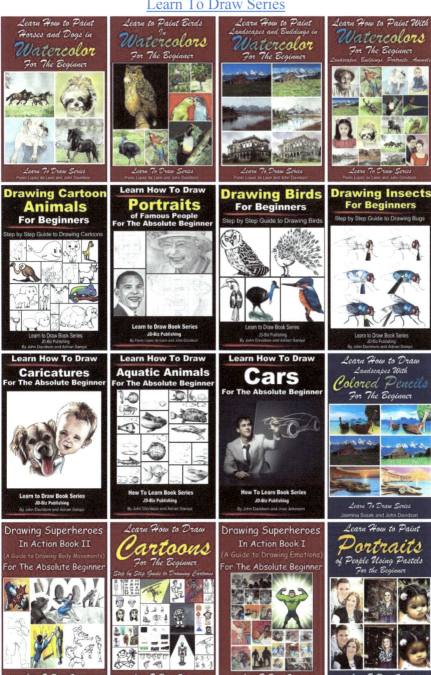

Our books are available at

1. Amazon.com

2. Barnes and Noble

3. Itunes

4. Kobo

5. Smashwords

6. Google Play Books

Download Free Books!
http://MendonCottageBooks.com

Publisher

JD-Biz Corp

P O Box 374

Mendon, Utah 84325

http://www.jd-biz.com/

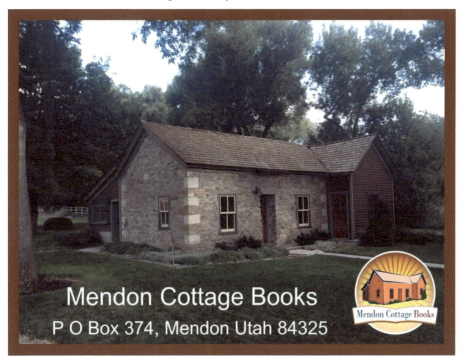